GOD **SEEKING**

Revelations of Beauty and Truth

by John Smed

Copyright © 2025 by John F. Smed

Published by Prayer Current
106 – 1033 Haro Street
Vancouver, BC V6E 1C8
CANADA

All rights reserved.

No part of this publication may be reproduced, stored in a retrieval system, or transmitted in any form or by any means – electronic, mechanical, photocopy, recording, or any other – except for brief quotations in printed reviews, without the prior permission of the publisher.

MET BY GOD

Forward: What is a spiritual quest?

Introduction: Lost and missing in New York

Chapter 1. Noticed

Chapter 2. Is That All There is?

Chapter 3. Summiting

Chapter 4. The Stars are Singing

Chapter 5. Jekyll and Hyde

Chapter 6. The Hounds of Heaven

Chapter 7. A Siren Sounds

Chapter 8. There is Something About that Name

Chapter 9. Going It Alone

Chapter 10. The Endless Circle

Chapter 11. Back to the Garden

Postscript

FOREWORD

"God seeking" can have different meanings. On the one hand, the seeker is the subject who is doing the seeking. On the other hand, if God is the subject, then God is the One doing the seeking. In this narrative I have both in mind.

My story is about a troubled teen who finds God. I write to reflect on what it means to be met by God and how it comes about. There is no blueprint here, but my personal experiences contain some universal truths that can help others start and then navigate their own journey.

Over my early to mid-teen years, I ascend from deep darkness to radiant light.

Plato taught that the difference between being ignorant and knowing is the difference between shadow and reality. He uses the example of someone born and raised in a cave. Because the cave dweller lives in darkness, as he begins to ascend, he encounters reflected light from the entrance above. Now he lives in a world of shadows. Only when he leaves the cave and moves into the light of day does the cave dweller leave the realm of shadows and gain a direct understanding of the world. This journey from darkness, to shadow, and into the light is what philosophy is all about.

Whatever means we use to climb out from our cave, we do not have to navigate our ascent solo. Another descends into our benighted world to draw us to daylight. Left to ourselves, we would still be lost in a world of shadows, cave dwellers still.

There are two halves to reality- seen and unseen, with only a thin veil between. Remove the veil, and both sides are revealed as one. God's descent into my world ends with my ascent to God's world, as he lifts me from my earth-bound self to unseen and eternal realms.

God comes to me. He draws me into his realm. I discover God as He reveals Himself to me. Another seeker, a guilt-ridden slave trading sailor, while battered by a gale, was less philosophical and more desperate.

> *I once was lost but now am found,*
> *Was blind but now I see.*
> —John Newton

During my teen years, I have several overwhelming revelations. My blind eyes were opened to see. The veil was lifted, and an ever-present reality lay before me. Up to now, I simply didn't have eyes to see. More to the point- I did not want to see. I needed to be cornered and herded toward the light, or I would simply run back and hide in my cave.

Plato argued that knowledge is recollection. When I meet God, it is déjà vu. At some level of consciousness, I already knew him. In our created origins, we are imprinted with knowledge of God. When someone encounters God, they recognize what they already know. A light goes on. Darkness is dispelled. An ever-present reality lies open to view.

Beyond Plato's reflections, my spiritual quest is more than gaining a consciousness of what is absolute- it is a relational reality.

In each chapter, I share my revelations of awe, beauty, and truth. I confess my futile and painful attempts to ascend to peace, joy, and fulfillment apart from God.

Quotes and references are from revered ancient sources. I've also included lyrics from songs and books that were written around the time of my journey. It was late fall of the hippie revolution. A generation was in the middle of a mini-renaissance of creativity- especially in its music and songs.

All along my quest, the music echoes in my soul, providing fertile soil for my explorations.

You may ask a fair question; *"How can you remember these experiences, with such detail and clarity—some fifty years later"?*

I've done my very best to recount my experiences truthfully, the revelations and epiphanies. However, more importantly, there is something about being met by God that leaves an indelible and permanent mark on the retina of my soul. It is not just a matter of how retentive my long-term memory is, there is a profound and timeless permanence to those experiences. In a most literal sense, encounters with God are unforgettable.

INTRODUCTION: LOST AND MISSING IN NEW YORK

It's 1958. I'm five years old, two thousand miles from home and completely lost in downtown Brooklyn- a city of more than a million people. In four hours, I'm supposed to board the Queen Mary with my family. Dad, mom, and we four kids drove to New York to sail to Denmark where my parents and siblings emigrated from seven years earlier.

The night before embarking we stayed with Danish friends in Brooklyn. Their little boy wouldn't share his five-cent candy necklace with me. Nickle in hand, I head out to find my own. After a determined search down several streets, I can't locate a store. I lose my bearings. I gaze up at tall apartment buildings, they all look the same. I don't know which way to turn or where to find help to get back home. I've never been in Brooklyn so there is no chance of finding landmarks. I need to be found.

Holding back tears I wander up one street after another. Coming around a corner, I spot a policeman. He spots me. He comes directly up to me, takes me by the hand and guides me to the precinct.

He books me and tells me to sit on a corner bench. Enclosed by wooden rails and a gate, ice cream and jail cats share my confinement. In about twenty minutes, my dad comes and bails me out. Everyone is relieved. I find my way home. Later that day, we board ship to Denmark.

There is a vast difference between being lost and being lost and missing. It turns out that I was not only lost, but I was also missing. Imagine you are on a hike and stray off the trail into dense woods. You hadn't notified anyone where you were going so there is no one able to search for you. Now that's a whole different kind of lost.

As soon as they knew I had wandered away, my dad and mom went on the hunt. They put out the APB and nothing else matters. When they found me, they weren't angry that I wandered away—they were excited to find me.

I say, *"I found my way home".* For a five-year-old, this seems the case. The truth is, I'm found. Alerted to me being lost, the police officer was looking for me. He heard that a little boy was lost in a big city. He knew the clock was ticking. He was looking for me before I was looking for him.

This parallels my personal quest. I imagine that I find God. It turns out he finds me. In the pages ahead I share the zigzag journey.

My experience in Brooklyn lasts only a few hours. At first, this lost boy does not want to be found. I was on a quest—it was for something silly, but something important to me. I needed to realize that I was lost before I could be found.

It is the same with my spiritual journey. It takes a few years. At first, I don't want to be found. I'm pursuing silly things—they used to call it folly. At first, I'm not ready to be found. I see God before me, but I turn and head down another street…

Like a little boy lost in the world and lost in self, I find God because he seeks me out again and again. It turns out this is how it works. God initiates the search. He lifts the veil. He does the finding.

Jesus says, *'Seek and you will find'.* In my seeking I discover that God is on the hunt. He interrupts the course of my life, one awe-filled experience after another.

CHAPTER 1 • NOTICED

Look intently at someone. Hold that gaze. Invariably, they turn to see who is staring at them. Somehow, we know when someone really pays attention to us. We love to be noticed- especially by someone we look up to. My childhood memories have faded, lost in the confusion and tumult of a world I didn't understand. However, one memory lingers. I feel unnoticed.

I recall a black and white childhood photo of me standing beside my father. I'm three or four years old, holding onto his pant leg. My father looks straight ahead as if into the future. I look down and to the side. I avert my eyes, as if unsure if I fit in the picture. I live on the periphery of his vision.

It's still painful to look at this picture. I feel myself fading into the background. Uncertain where I belong, I wonder why I'm in the picture at all.

I don't hold this neglect against my father. (We become friends years later). I understand why work commands his attention. My father is a new immigrant. He pours his life into this new world. Like any pioneer, clearing a path and building a future, exhausts his time and energy. There's little of either left for a child born the year after they land.

If one word describes my childhood, it is 'unnoticed'. Perhaps this is why I have so few recollections of that time. Memories need fixed points to build on, anchors to hold them in place. Locating self is not only an inner journey. You need others to help you find your place in life. I need a father to notice me. Without a father's recognition, I disappear into the surrounding world. I'll spend the rest of my life trying to find where I belong.

It's not just actors and musicians that want to be discovered. We all long to be accepted, approved, and acknowledged- we all want to be known. As I grow, I search. Like most everyone, I seek attention. Wanting to be known, I look this way and that, trying to fit in, hoping to be noticed.

I wake from my slumbers

When I turn thirteen, like every son of the Lutheran church, I attend confirmation classes. These classes last twelve weeks and are held early Saturday morning in the basement of Shepherd King Lutheran Church. Unsought and unexpected, one of these mornings, God comes to me. One minute, I'm half-awake, my head l resting on my elbow. I'm scarcely listening. The next, I'm jolted into cosmic clarity. Something massive enters, fills, and then slowly passes by.

God notices the least and ignores the proud. Recall the Christmas story. God appears to mangy shepherds. "Suddenly the glory of the Lord shone around them." One minute, they're minding the sheep, the next, they're surrounded by God and a legion chorus of mighty angels. The least of all people, they're struck dumb that God would notice them. I am about to have the same experience.

Seven other thirteen and fourteen-year-olds attend the class. My guess is only one or two have a clue why we are here. We are certainly not looking for God. Charlie Beefus, the only one in the class I know, quits after a few weeks. The pastor seems bored and frustrated by our inattentiveness. Teaching teens is a tedious duty. His attitude is catching- I'm bored too.

I come by my spiritual lethargy honestly. I'm brought up in secular times. My parents never question the prevailing unbelief of our time. God and faith belong to the realm of tradition and wish fulfillment, not truth or reality. Not believing in God is normal. Faith is unusual. Charles Taylor wrote about our secular world:

> *"...why was it virtually impossible not to believe in God in, say, 1500 in our Western Society, while in 2000 many of*

us find this is not only easy but inescapable.?"

Catechumens are required to memorize questions and answers from Luther's catechism. Once we can recite the Ten Commandments, the Apostle's Creed, and the Lord's Prayer, we graduate and take our first communion. Actual belief or comprehension is assumed but not required. I do my homework. It's a mild penance for the gifts that will attend my first communion. I'll get a Bible from my parents and cash presents from well-wishing relatives.

Memorizing the catechism goes down without a hitch. However, nothing arrests my attention. I don't expect it to. I've given little thought to God. A few friends go to church, but no one I know talks or cares about these things. Mention God and you get a polite silence or dismissive comment. Reciting the Lord's Prayer in elementary school has been the extent of my religious instruction. Until this morning, there are no bells, no whistles, and no revelations.

Something massive enters the room

This Saturday, things are going to be different— irreversibly so. One minute the pastor is reading from Luther's Small Catechism, something about God's fatherhood and power.

> *With these words God tenderly invites us to believe that He is our true Father and that we are His true children, so that with all boldness and confidence we may ask Him as dear children ask their dear father.*

The next minute there's a pregnant pause in the space time continuum. A mountainous something enters and fills the room, the whole building, crowding the space from floor to ceiling, filling the air from basement to sanctuary.

I feel like Moses at the foot of Sanai- lightning, earthquake and all.

As the pastor drones on, instantly, I'm surrounded. The words grab me by the scruff- something new, alarming, inescapably true. I hear thunder roll off those pages.

Unexpected and unsought, I'm confronted with Majesty and Immensity in its pure fulness. I can't explain how—but I know I am being immersed in an All-Knowing Presence. I am experiencing the other and greater side of reality, a fifth dimension.

Luther's Small Catechism blindsides me. This ex-monk portrays a majestic and awesome God- a radical contrast between just thinking about God and believing in him.

> *Hallowed be Thy name. He that teaches and lives otherwise than God's Word teaches profanes the name of God among us. From this preserve us, Heavenly Father.*

Luther's exhortation doesn't turn me off, in fact the opposite. I'm drawn in. I long for this immense, living conception of Divinity. Somewhere in the inner recesses of my heart, I want the world to be sacred—not a barren wasteland; not an absurdity heading nowhere and meaning nothing. I don't have the words to express it, but I want to meet God.

One minute time creeps on its petty pace, then suddenly, the clock stops ticking. It may have lasted only a few seconds, but it felt timeless. My entire being, mind and body, is hooked, netted, and landed.

A new galactic reality descends into the orbit of my consciousness. Consider Jupiter. It is three hundred times the mass of earth. Were it to enter earth's orbit everything would change. Drawn into this immensity would either destroy Earth or set it on a whole new trajectory. God's presence has weight. The Hebrew word for glory is is 'kabod'. It means weight or heaviness. God is heavy. God is weighty.

In the book of Exodus, in the Mount Sinai episode, Moses asks

God, *"Show me your glory"*. Moses wants to feel the weight. God answers Moses' prayer. He says, *"I will allow my glory to pass by you".*

God hides Moses in a cleft of a rock, at the same time shielding him with his hand. Moses is only allowed to catch a glimpse of God's glory. Any more would crush him.

Moses wants to see God. Even more, he wants to be seen by God. Moses wants to know God. Even more, he wants to be known by God. Like everyone, Moses wants to be noticed.

That morning, I felt something that Moses felt. Suddenly, God passes by. I feel the enormity of His holy being. I glimpse the edge of his splendor. I'm conscious of another Consciousness. I know that I'm being gazed at. Someone is aware of me. For a serene and awesome moment, I'm entirely open and laid bare. I'm not embarrassed. I'm noticed.

Experiencing this immense Otherness of God sets up a before-and-after. Before everything is one-dimensional-bland and ordinary. From this moment on, my universe has expanded, I experience unseen dimensions that will steadily grow in my awareness until the supernatural eclipses the natural.

Yanked out of my indifference, I'm drawn in- towards a Being that I will one day become a part of. I'm not in yet, but from that moment on, I know I want in.

Then, suddenly as it came, the Presence lifts, departs, and life returns to ordinary. Or, I wonder, perhaps is it I that leave? Steeped in the mundane, I have a short attention span for numinous experiences.

"What just happened?", I look around. What seemed hours to me, was just a moment to the others. The other kids still look bored. I look up to the pastor. I ask him to repeat the words. He does and his tone doesn't change. No one else has

experienced this revelation.

After class, I go home and tell my mother, "I think I might be a minister someday". This is a strange comment for a fourteen-year-old. My mother smiles and says, "That would make Grandpa happy."

Simone Weil says, *"Only two things pierce the human heart. One is beauty. The other is affliction."* I just experienced the first. I'm about to experience the second.

CHAPTER 2 • IS THAT ALL THERE IS?

> *Is that all there is?*
> *Is that all there is?*
> *If that's all there is my friends*
> *Then let's keep dancing*
> *Let's break out the booze and have a ball*
> *If that's all there is.*
>
> —Peggy Lee 1969

As I look back at my upbringing, Dad wasn't harsh or uncaring. Raised in a poor family of nine children in rural Denmark, he had to leave school after grade five and work full-time as a cabinetmaker's apprentice. For Kai Smed, school was a luxury, work a necessity.

When Granddad was seriously injured, he couldn't work. With no social welfare in Denmark at the time, my grandparents had to rely on neighbors' charity. Grandma also made a few kroners a day harvesting peat moss, which is dried and used for stove fuel. She packed up her nine children and headed to the fields. Older kids looked after the younger, including the baby, and my blind uncle Laurits. One day while grandma worked, the older girls were distracted, and Laurits crawled into a pool. The folklore is that he was found miraculously floating on the surface of the pond.

When my parents emigrate from Denmark to Canada, Dad makes good. He works his way up to become a shop foreman. Later, he runs and manages his own cabinet shop. Understandably, Dad thinks it's a good idea for his boys to follow his path. When we turn eleven, we're expected to work. This means long days- every Saturday, some Sundays, and all summer. What was good for Dad will be good for us.

While my friends contemplate mischief and enjoy summer

holidays, I'm hauled off to the shop to put in a fifty-hour work week. Summertime is workin' time. Except for a one-week family vacation, a six-day workweek through July and August is expected. *"You don't argue with Dad."*

Becoming a *hard worker* is my parents' measuring stick. How I spend my time outside work is my own business. Unlike my brothers, I had no interest in going fishing with Dad on his day off. He already highjacked enough of my time.

Robbed of the fun my friends are having, I do everything I can to avoid work. I linger and I dawdle, dragging my feet. I even try to hide in the sawdust bin. I come to realize avoiding work is more trouble than working, so I give in. I resign myself to the routines of the work-a-day world. Up at 6:00, I work from 7:30 in the morning to 6:00 in the evening. I punch the time clock when I arrive and depart. A loud *blannngggnzzz!!* signals a ten-minute coffee or a thirty-minute lunch.

> *Up at eight, you can't be late*
> *for Matthew & Son, he won't wait...*
> *There's a five-minute break and that's all you take,*
> *for a cup of cold coffee and a piece of cake...*
> —Cat Stevens, *Matthew and Son 1966*

Even a twelve-year-old realizes that a day's hard work isn't going to kill him. It feels good to do a job and do it well. I learn cabinet-making skills. I enjoy watching craftsmen take wood, veneer, glue, and screws, and make a fine piece of furniture. In the paint-room, I sand desks, bookcases, and boardroom tables. Lacquer turns plain wood grain into beautiful displays of flame. I spend time in the paint shop with Carl, a gentle old Danish soul who has nothing but patience for an unhappy kid. He walks through life and work with a gentle piety. He's gone now, but I remember him with deep affection.

I do my time for the next ten years—six days dressing planks or driving truck and cleaning the shop on weekends. I know I don't want to follow my father's path. I respect him, even admire him, but his story is not my story. My father wakes up irritable and goes to bed grumpy. Dad knew how to have fun, but the dream of getting ahead through hard work is all-consuming.

Whenever I imagine following my father's example, I get depressed. If that's all there is, I see futility.

> *Vanity of vanities! All is vanity.*
> *What does man gain by all the toil*
> *at which he toils under the sun?*
>
> —Solomon, *Ecclesiastes*

I don't want to live my life by someone else's script. Something deep within calls, an inner longing that is part self-determination and part rebellion, but there is more to it. A homing device beckons me to another plan and another destiny.

Up until now, all the world seems black and white. I'm looking for color. When I look to the future, I only see a bland horizon. I want to see the rising sun of a new day. The soul abhors a vacuum. Good or bad, our spirit will dive into a dream and follow a vision. As I erase my dad's story from my soul, the void cries out. The psalmist says, 'Deep calls to deep'. I head down another path and into another dream. Like Alice in Wonderland, I dive down a rabbit hole and enter a fantastical world. It's a free fall and a miracle if I ever get out.

My serious explorations begin Christmas 1969. I'm sixteen. Our family travels to San Francisco. We're visiting friends, the Christiansen family, cousins from the *old country*. They live in Sausalito, just up the hill from the Haight and Ashbury.

It's the tail-end of the hippie renaissance. Cracks appear in the dream. Woodstock writes its own obituary. Soon Jimmy Hendrix, Janis Joplin, and Jim Morrison will be dead- each at

27. The Vietnam War drags on- a cultural headache turned nightmare. Joan Baez laments a *'generation of no tomorrows'*. Dylan sings, *'The times they are a changin'.* A few idealists hold on, trying to squeeze hope from depleted dreams. They smoked their dream- now all that is left is ashes.

One night, I go down to town with my cousin Tommy. We descend steep winding roads to the town below. As we approach the center, Tommy opens his wallet and dips into the change slot. He brings out three rolled 'cigarettes'. *"Hey John, want to smoke these with me?"*

At first, I don't get it. It takes a minute. I look at Tommy's knowing smile. Finally, it dawns on me. *"Hey, this is marijuana!"* At the time, where I come from, even carrying weed is a felony. I'm scared- at the same time I feel the pull of the unknown and the thrill of the forbidden. *"Smoke this and your story changes."* The minute I lay my eyes on those joints, I know I'm going to smoke them. It's irresistible.

Tommy takes a long toke and holds the joint out to me. I take it and inhale deeply. Lungs filled and sinuses burning, choking, I stifle a cough. *"Hmm! I like it."* I inhale again- and again- and again. *"Now that's really different!"* It's partly scary, partly sacred. *"So, this is where it's at... and I like it!"*

I plummet head-first into a whirling tunnel. Later, I'll drop acid. I'll even try speed a few times. The way down churns up my subconscious. It's called a trip for good reasons. It reminds me of the feeling you get when you jump off a high ledge into a dark pool of water.

One sunny afternoon in grade ten I head to Glenmore Dam with a bunch of high school friends. We look down a dizzy twelve meters to a deep reservoir. One at a time, we take turns jumping off the bridge. The water's clean but so deep it's black. Hidden beneath the surface are vertically suspended logs- dead heads. You can't see them. Hit one going in—you'll break a leg or worse. For a teenager surrounded by friends, the danger adds to the adventure. Signs warn, "No jumping!" The thrill of the height, the danger of the logs, the fact that it's illegal makes it perfect. *"Geronimo!"* I jump. I swallow my heart. It takes forever. I brace and plunge down. Luck is on my side. Surfacing, I yell, *"It's freezing!"*

That moment in Sausalito, as I inhale it all in, I'm gripped with anticipation, *"Maybe this is more."* Tommy's grass doesn't take me far. Still, I've enough THC in me to parrot the lingo all night long…*"Yeah cool!" "Far out man!" "Peace brother!"* I'm sure Tommy thinks I'm a bit of a dolt. Still, he smiles. He likes his little cuz'.

That night in Sausalito, it turns out the great Jefferson Airplane is playing. In their repertoire, lead singer Grace Slick belts out a tune that puts words to my experience:

> And if you go chasing rabbits
> And you know you're going to fall
> Tell them a hookah-smoking caterpillar
> Has given you the call
> —White Rabbit 1971

Grace Slick and other minstrels of mayhem invite me into a new narrative. As they drum, strum, and wail- the underlying beat penetrates my soul. I inhale it- deeply.

I like this new world. It's an exhilarating alternative to an absurd and banal life. It is an altered reality. Pot and partying expand my mind, but things begin to come apart. It won't be long before I find myself in a deeper hole than I reckoned. Climbing out is going to be harder than diving down. Tripping becomes downright dangerous.

I recall another experience at Glenmore Dam. On one side we jump. On the other side we careen down a thirty-five-meter spill way. A steady trickle of water overflows the dam running down where the sloped wall meets the side wall. It is super slick with green scum. The slide is only a few degrees shy of vertical. It makes for a luge-like descent into turbulent waters. One night, after quaffing a half dozen at a pub, five of us climb into my 59 Chevy- the 'Blue Goose'. We head to the spillway for a midnight slide. We all swim well- except Colin.

There are warning signs all over the place. Because of changing outflow from the dam, currents can be dangerous. Ripping down, plunging into the pool, after you come up for air you need to swim fifty meters to where you climb out. There's nothing to cling to, so there's no way back. You must be a good swimmer.

This night something is ominously different. We fail to notice the side vent is wide open and tons of water cascade out, creating a massive whirlpool. The current against us is going to be two or three times stronger than usual.

Greg and Gary go first. Ignorant and heedless I follow. I careen down and blast into the whirling waters. Coming up for air, I realize I'm fighting an overwhelming current. Still, there is no option but to swim to where I can climb out. It doesn't help that I've been drinking.

Colin follows. I look back. As soon as he surfaces, I can see he's struggling. He makes it less than half-way to safety and begins to flail. I see fear in his eyes. I don't know what to do. I barely have enough strength to get to safety myself. I can't carry Colin. I drift back with the current and try to push him forward. It doesn't help. Now we are all scared- in earnest. We start to panic, *"Colin is going to drown."* Without help, he will.

Mike shoots down. He's a summer lifeguard- thank God. He swims up and grabs Colin with a rescue hold and slowly pulls him to safety. We dodged a bullet.

As I slide down the current of pot and partying, I plunge into the turbulence. I soon discover I can't just stop- the way back is closed. I take reckless chances. I make stupid choices. Pretty soon, I'll be over my head—struggling against the current of a bad conscience and broken relationships. Like my friend Colin, I will need rescuing.

CHAPTER 3 • SUMMITTING

Leaving my father's vision behind, I start on a new path. I begin exploring pleasure in earnest. I want to get higher- not only to get stoned, but also to break through the clouds to the other side of this flat, bland world. I want to summit beyond the absurdity of the now.

My brief catechism meeting with God fades into memory. For a few moments I had surfaced above the seen world to the eternal world. Yet over time I subside back into the closed world of self and sense.

I meet pot and pot meets me. For much of the next three years, *smokin'* and *tokin'* clouds my world. At first it seems a great adventure. I have some fun. I learn some things. I make new friends who are part of the scene. Eventually other friends join in. However, most of the time they just want to get wasted. I'm disappointed by their lack of imagination. I like to get high too, but for me there has to be more to it.

I wonder how anyone can be happy with the world as it is. I don't mean the wars, troubles, and disasters of life. I mean, how can anyone be content in a world without meaning, without hope, and without awe? I have a rooted sadness growing within. I want to escape it. I also want to replace it.

I feel as if I'm at the base of some great mountain. I want to find a way to escape the bland futility of fate. Like a high mountain climber, I'm at base camp and eager to get to the next stage.

Holy men take to a mountain-top to connect with another realm. They ascend beyond earth-bound realities. They isolate from the din of the crowd. Breathing thin, cold air clears the mind and cleanses the spirit. Words become unnecessary. They find something in the heights the valleys can never offer.

On Mount Sinai, God reveals his very being to Moses. Shrouded in smoke, thunder, lightning and blasting trumpets, God breaks through to be seen. Moses brings seventy elders with him. They lift their eyes to see a vision of God.

> *The seventy elders of Israel went up and saw the God of Israel. Under his feet was something like a pavement made of lapis lazuli, as bright blue as the sky.*
> —Exodus 24:1-17

If I'm going to find some of that thunder and lightning, I'm going to need to climb a mountain. Briefly, I imagine that I might make the climb by smoking pot. It turns out I've no idea the force required to escape earth's gravity.

Like Moses and his seventy, I recruit a team for the quest. I use pot as relational currency. I share my stash. I despise those who bogart their joints. I turn others on- hoping they will join in. A team will have a greater chance of summitting.

One night in my parent's rumpus room, five of us form a circle and hold hands. The music is loud and pulsing with rhythm. We are carried upward in clouds of smoke. We sway back and forth, entering a kind of trance. There is a deep current between us. As the music fades into the background, we enter a timeless moment. It's a roughshod communion of sorts.

I start to sing *I Want to Take You Higher* by Sly and the Family Stone and all join in. We rock back and forth. We look at each other, smiling and happy to be in this place and to be together.

Looking around at the faces of my friends, I search their eyes. I look for signs of awakening. *Something* is within reach. We come close. It is near enough to touch but too far to enter.

Suddenly the music dies. We fall to earth. There is simply not enough faith-momentum to keep us together- not sufficient power to get us to where we want to go. Encouraged that we ascended, yet disappointed it was over, each one wanders home with a memory. Coming down is disheartening.

Trying to ascend to another realm is not unlike climbing a mountain. The way up is difficult. The way down can be even more difficult.

The movie *North Face* is taken from a true story. It's about a climbing a mountain. Really, it's about descending. The Eiger is a 3,970-meter (13,020 ft) mountain of the Bernese Alps, overlooking the town of Grindelwald. At 2,866 meters, carved into the side of the mountain is the Eigerwand railway viewpoint- providing a spectacular south-facing view. The north face is 1400 meters of sheer granite cliff. In 1935, several teams of climbers compete to scale the north face. It has never been accomplished.

Two teams of four set out. The focus is on the German team. Their ascent quickly becomes hazardous. A climber is injured on the way up. Then things turn ugly. As they begin the emergency descent, a vicious storm with freezing winds blows in. Conditions worsen and they're forced to bivouac overnight against the cliff and fully exposed to freezing winds.

While they wait out the storm, the situation turns deadly. Another member of their team slips. He is left hanging mid-air, threatening to bring others down with him. To save the others he cuts his own rope and falls to his death. Then the first injured climber dies. In extreme and worsening conditions, another climber succumbs. Only one of the German team is left.

Desperate, this climber has one last hope. He must rappel to the gouged-out railway viewpoint mid-way down the mountain. It might possibly be within reach. At the outset of his struggle, the climber loses a glove. Within minutes, his hand freezes solid. He doesn't give up. Hope beyond hope he starts to swing himself back and forth, extending his rope, each time getting closer and closer to the cleft in the rock. After superhuman effort he comes almost within reach. A few meters from safety, he runs out of rope. Grimly, desperately, he tries to braid more. Again, he swings side to side, now within a few feet of safety.

Tragically, the knot in the braided rope gets snagged in the climbing ring. With bleeding, frozen fingers, he strains to lift himself over the knot. He tries again and again. With a final gasp he collapses, surrendering to the icy and indifferent forces of the mountain.

The night five of us try to ascend. We get close enough to touch the beyond. Sadly, we find ourselves suspended between a very real earth and a too distant heaven. We try to summit but have neither resources nor strength to pull it off.

It turns out I've no idea what it takes to break through the clouds and escape the earth's gravity. Scientists tell us that for a rocket it's Mach 33 (33 times the speed of sound). For a person who weighs 100 kilograms, this would require the power of 30 Concorde jets on each foot.

I didn't know it at the time, but someday I'll be empowered for the ascent. In the meantime, I get nearer and nearer to the end of my rope. Before I collapse and surrender to gravity, I'll be sustained by another surprising revelation.

CHAPTER 4 • THE STARS ARE SINGING!

Van Gogh, Starry Night

At present we are on the outside of the world, the wrong side of the door. We discern the freshness and purity of morning, but they do not make us fresh and pure. We cannot mingle with the splendors we see. But all the leaves of the New Testament are rustling with the rumor that it will not always be so. Someday, God willing, we shall get in.
—C.S. Lewis, *The Weight of Glory*

The heavens declare the glory of God;
the skies proclaim the work of his hands.
Day after day they pour forth speech;
night after night they reveal knowledge.
They have no speech, they use no words;
no sound is heard from them.
Yet their voice goes out into all the earth,
their words to the ends of the world.
—Psalm 19

Like a cash strapped teen who puts a few dollars into the tank at a time, I live off fumes. I near the end of my reckless ways, but still very much earth-bound. I'm beginning to realize that my present trajectory will never take me where I long go. If I'm going to transcend the visible, the invisible will have to come to me.

One mid-summer night, I head out with friends far from the city lights to the rolling foothills. We decide to spend the night under the stars. We smoke pot, drink beer- and *other stuff.* The *other stuff* increases the risk and the adventure. It also accelerates my free fall. Free fall is measured as ten meters per second squared. In other words, the further you fall the faster you go. When you reach terminal velocity, the crash will be terminal too.

We park off a side road and make our way up the hill through a thick glade of trees. Crossing through to the other side, we enter a meadow and a spectacular vista- a collage of rolling hills and a river valley scattered with trees, bushes and clearings between. The sun has set, and stars begin to light the sky. We settle down on a grassy slope. We smoke. We drink. We get high. The pure indigo sky is laced with a canopy of stars- extending to a galactic forever.

We talk about friendship, life, girls- whatever. We enjoy our kinship- partly real, partly induced. We chatter past midnight. One by one, my companions nod off where they lie. Not me. Not tonight. I'm wide-awake. I'm in a state of crystal awareness.

Perched in the middle of that meadow, in the silent stillness I enter the real and the imagined. The hillside becomes an amphitheater. The night sky becomes a canvas. I lay back and gaze horizon to horizon and the radiance between. I can't stop staring at the kaleidoscopic heavens. The stars pulsate as if alive. Captured by the beauty—I feel an exquisite pain,

> *Some kind of ecstasy got a hold on me.*
> —Bruce Coburn

Maybe Van Gogh, in his heightened imbalance, experienced something similar.

An audience of one, I enjoy a symphony of fire and light. While sleep envelopes the world the sky is fully awake. The night is silent, but the stars are singing their ancient song. I attend a cosmic concert. Fiery lights take their positions, in glorious choral array.

The night deepens. I'm drawn further in, immersed in splendor. I lose all sense of time. I don't feel alone. I share the sacred awareness of Jacob as he sits under the stars at Bethel.

> *God is surely in this place*
> *—Genesis 28:16*

The Greek word for revelation is apocalypse. It means to draw the curtain back and open heaven to view. This starry night, heaven opens, and I enter in. The veil is lifted, and I see what eyes were made to see.

Faith expands out of the narrow confines of self-deception. Unbelief buries its head in the sand. Faith is coming up for air. I think of the prophet Elisha, who prays for God to open eyes to the fiery realities surrounding him:

> *Then Elisha prayed and said, "O Lord, please open his eyes that he may see." So the Lord opened the eyes of the young man, and he saw, and behold, the mountain was full of horses and chariots of fire all around Elisha.*
> *—2 Kings 6:17-20*

Stars image God. Their fire is inexhaustible—without beginning and without end—fueling billion-year fires. Fission fragments the elements; fusion brings them together. The power of our star is such that only two parts in a million of the sun's radiant heats and sustains all life on earth. From God's infinite reserves, His glory sustains everything, giving light to every soul.

Minutes pass into hours. Deep passes into deep. Waiting,

observing, receiving, I'm experiencing a sliver of eternity. I want this moment to sink in; I want to sink into this moment.

King David sings *"I will shout. I will awaken the dawn!"* I shout. I sing. Unbidden, from within me, comes a song, loud and clear. I echo a word over and over. It's my first prayer.

> *Amen, amen, amen, amen, amen*
> *Sing it over!*
> *Amen. Amen. Amen, amen, amen.*

The song comes from Lilies of the Field, a popular movie released in 1963 about a black man, Homer Smith, who is traveling cross country in search of a living. He comes upon a simple settlement of German nuns. They're trying to set up a convent community in the wilderness. Homer is short on cash, and could use a meal and a bed, so he offers to do some chores. The nuns share their meager meals and give him a place to sleep.

Each evening Homer plans to leave to leave the next day Something keeps him from going. After several days, the Mother Superior conscripts him. She says, "Schmidt, God says, 'You build us a 'shappel'!' "No way, sister!" he says. But Homer can't help himself. He starts to care for these hapless nuns and builds them a *shappel*.

At one mealtime, they ask him to pray. Homer teaches the nuns the chorus of an old negro spiritual. He sings a line. They repeat it. At first, they don't get it, but as the song progresses, they join in with perfect joy and harmony.

> *Amen... Amen...Amen!*
> *Sing it over!*
> *Amen... Amen... Amen!*

My heart repeats the chorus, "Amen, Amen, Amen!"

The sky is pregnant with light and I'm bathing in it. I merge with the splendor and fire. The joy in my soul is a kind of applause. I can't help it. I sing out loud and long. I'm giving thanks for the splendor of the heavens. God is in the very air.

> *Do heaven and earth contain the whole of you, since you fill them? Are you present entirely everywhere at once, and no single part contains the whole of you?*
> —Augustine

This antiphony of sky and heart goes on for hours. I happen upon the singing which starts after midnight. Now, as stars fade and the music subsides, dawn creases the horizon. My soul comes to rest.

I recall the words of another Negro spiritual and give thanks with a song. In a full spirit of appreciation and supplication, I sway as I sing:

> *Swing low, sweet chariot,*
> *Comin' for to carry me home;*
> *Swing low, sweet chariot,*
> *Comin' for to carry me home.*
>
> *I looked over Jordan,*
> *And WHAT did I see,*
> *Comin' for to carry me home,*
> *A band of angels comin' after me,*
> *Comin' for to carry me home.*

As the stars die, the blue of the sky expands. The thin line of dawn rises and outlines the hills. As the new day dawns, I'm content to be me in this place.

I'm sure the *other stuff* heightens my awareness. Yet, as the evening progresses, I'm sober. I know because I don't crash later. A deep sense of well-being continues for days.

One or two nights a week, for the rest of the summer, I perch myself on a hillside by the Glenmore Reservoir. I face the mountains. I watch the sky. I look for singing stars and am not disappointed. It is a special summer. As if on cue, stars marshal into choral formation. They sing the night away until morning dawns.

CHAPTER 5 • JEKYLL AND HYDE

All things therefore seemed to point to this: that I was slowly losing hold of my original and better self, and becoming slowly incorporated with my second and worse.
—Robert Louis Stevenson
  The Strange Case of Dr. Jekyll and Mr. Hyde

So far, I've had two God sightings. In my Saturday morning catechism class, I feel the gravity of an unseen Immensity. I enter a quantum shift- beyond space and time, beyond natural to supernatural. I am noticed.

Under the singing stars my eyes open. It is a revelation that the heavens and earth are filled with Presence. Still to come, I will hear an alarming voice, even a shout, in the fog. I'll be overwhelmed by an apocalyptic sense of my lostness- jolted from nameless guilt to real conviction. The daily decisions of life morph from mundane to momentous.

Despite these epiphanies, darker thoughts continue to rise from within, climbing from a buried conscience. I'm hounded by a sense of wrongness. Pleasure seeking runs its course and cries out for a reckoning. On the canvas of my journey, the manifest brilliance highlights the darkness within. God invites me to ascend above my earthbound life. Yet, something still holds me back, holds me down.

I was greedy to enjoy what the world had to offer, though it only eluded me and wasted my strength...Why then do I delay? Why do I not abandon my worldly hopes and give myself entirely to the search for God and true happiness...? But not so fast! This life is too sweet. It has its own charms. They are of no small account and a man must not lightly undertake to detach his mind from them, because to return to them later would be a disgrace.
—Augustine *The Confessions*

I search. I avoid. Like a magnet, my heart has attraction forces, flip it over and it has repulsion forces. I want to unite with God. I also want my own way. Inside is a continual battle. My seeking self is trumped by baser realities. I'm Dr. Jekyll. I'm also Mr. Hyde.

In the *Strange Case of Dr. Jekyll and Mr. Hyde*, Robert Louis Stevenson describes the conflicting passions in every heart. At any given time, one side or the other dominates. Dr. Jekyll is an intelligent, courteous, well to do doctor. He is capable of deep affection and is surrounded by his friends. Mr. Hyde is the opposite. He is impulsive, fierce, proud, violent, explosive in hatred and anger. He has no friends, nor desires any.

The macabre part of the story is that Jekyll and Hyde are one and the same person. When good Dr. Jekyll takes a potion, it transforms him into evil Mr. Hyde. Evil is summoned.

> *This familiar [spirit]… I called out of my own soul… and sent forth to do his good pleasure…*

Jekyll has always enjoyed his secret sins

> *…it was as an ordinary secret sinner, that I at last fell before the assaults of temptation…*

While experimenting with his darker self, Jekyll believes he can maintain his civil self—his wealth, prestige, and friends.

At the same time, Jekyll revels in the pure evil of Hyde:

> *There was something strange in my sensations, something indescribably new and, from its very novelty, incredibly sweet. I felt younger, lighter, happier in body; within I was conscious of a heady recklessness, a current of disordered sensual images running like a millrace in my fancy, a solution of the bonds of obligation, an unknown but not an innocent freedom of the soul. I knew myself, at the first breath of this*

new life, to be more wicked, tenfold more wicked, sold a slave to my original evil; and the thought, in that moment, braced and delighted me like wine.

Dr. Jekyll's steps lead to a road of no return. Good is undeniable, but evil offers powerful and seductive compensation. The civility of Jekyll is no match for the incredible elation he experiences when he throws off constraint and gives free reign to his darker passions.

There is a moral to the story. Stevenson unmasks the lie that civil goodness has power over evil, and that good people can avoid evil whenever they choose. Under cover of darkness, we find our true selves. Remove the barrier of propriety, and Mr. Hyde will surface. The more rein we give to Mr. Hyde, the less we see of Dr. Jekyll.

This is not just a horror story. Stevenson's novella cut like a scalpel through the thin veneer of the time. Hyde-like realities are the sub-stratum beneath Victorian uprightness and civility. The book speaks to his time. Selling tens of thousands of copies in a matter of months, even Queen Victoria reads and approves it.

I apply this parable to myself as a sixteen-year-old, my Jekyll is no match for my Hyde. Reckless ways are fueled by dark passions within. In the late sixties, social constraints wear thin. Heedless of others, too often, we revel in sexual liberty. We call it free love. We imagine we can let loose our darkest passions and remain kind and civilized. Three Dog Night laments the sentiment, 'Easy to be hard. Easy to be cold.'

It's a trial-and-error experiment. Loyalty and fidelity are pitted against passion and lust. Something must give. The joys of friendship are overwhelmed by the base reality of lust. In fiery language Augustine nails what happens within:

> *I muddied the stream of friendship with the filth of lewdness and clouded its clear waters with Hell's black river of lust.*
> —Augustine *The Confessions*

Too willingly I ride the wave of self-indulgence. I give free reign to my passions. I know it's wrong. I have regrets. Morning remorse turns to nights excuses. I pursue my passion for pleasure in selfish and reckless ways. I'm consumed by this high-risk experiment until I hit a brick wall of conviction.

By God's grace, my conscience is not obliterated. A scarred faculty for right and wrong remains beneath Augustine's black river. I wake to regret my actions. My predations begin to prey on me. My eyes open to the brokenness and pain of those I've wounded and betrayed.

One day I walk by a girl in the halls of our high school. I could see pain and sadness in her eyes. It is the sorrow of my treachery. Her gaze is an indictment. Eyes tearing up, she shrinks back from me. I can't escape this diamond-hard reality. My felony stares me in the face—I'm shocked and embarrassed. I know I should be the one in tears.

> *So many hearts I find.*
> *Hearts like yours and mine.*
> *Torn by what we've done and can't undo.*
> —Leonard Cohen, Bernadette

In Stevenson's story, the more often he transforms, the stronger Hyde becomes. At first Jekyll is a riveted spectator of the remorseless Hyde. He can't turn away. However, the more frequently Jekyll takes the potion, he slowly drifts from spectator to agent. Jekyll becomes part of the scene.

> *.... Now, however, and in the light of that morning's accident, I was led to remark that whereas, in the beginning, the difficulty had been to throw off the body of Jekyll, it had of*

late, gradually but decidedly transferred itself to the other side. All things therefore seemed to point to this: that I was slowly losing hold of my original and better self and becoming slowly incorporated with my second and worse.

Yielding once too often, Jekyll becomes Hyde. He runs out of the potion that transforms him from Hyde back to Jekyll. Dismayed, he finds he can't recover the original formula.

The final horror of Stevenson's story is when Jekyll becomes Hyde without taking any potion. Listen to Jekyll's last words before he becomes Hyde forever:

Not that I dreamed of resuscitating Hyde; the bare idea of that would startle me to frenzy:
... There comes an end to all things... this brief condescension to evil finally destroyed the balance of my soul... It was a fine, clear, January day, wet under foot where the frost had melted, but cloudless overhead; and the Regent's Park was full of winter chirruping and sweet with spring odors. I sat in the sun on a bench; the animal within me licking the chops of memory; the spiritual side a little, drowsed, promising subsequent penitence, but not yet moved to begin. After all, I reflected, I was like my neighbors; and then I smiled, comparing myself with other men, comparing my active goodwill with the lazy cruelty of their neglect. And at the very moment of that vain-glorious thought, a qualm came over me, a horrid nausea and the most deadly shuddering. These passed away and left me faint; and then as in its turn the faintness subsided, I began to be aware of a change in the temper of my thoughts, a greater boldness, a contempt of danger, a solution of the bonds of obligation. I looked down; my clothes hung formlessly on my shrunken limbs; the hand that lay on my knee was corded and hairy. I was once more Edward Hyde. A moment before I had been safe of all men's respect, wealthy, beloved—the cloth laying for me in the dining-room at

home; and now I was the common quarry of mankind, hunted, houseless, a known murderer, thrall to the gallows.

Like Dr. Jekyll I have noble aspirations. I have friends that I value, men and women. At the same time, I have darker passions and ambitions that undermine everything good and tarnish every blessing.

I start as Dr. Jekyll—all kindness and conversation. When opportunity arises, darker passions take over. I am powerless to stop the marauding Mr. Hyde. I reap what I sow.

I suppress my conscience for a time, ignoring or avoiding those I injure. Eventually, my sins catch up and come back to haunt me. Betrayals large and small accumulate. Under the lash of a bad conscience, my soul wakes up. I thank God that I'm not permanently given over, not utterly beyond cure. I'm ready for strong medicine.

When guilt moves in, so does his cousin, shame. I've lived without shame for much of my adolescence. Now I feel my nakedness exposed.

I will come to understand that the guilt and shame are the necessary prelude to a new and truer self.

CHAPTER 6 • THE HOUNDS OF HEAVEN

Forget your perfect offering. There is a crack in everything. That's how the light gets in.
—Leonard Cohen, *Anthem*

I found my inner child. He's a bloody spoiled brat.
—Anonymous

If I squint, I can trace a thin edge of light on a distant horizon. However, once the light gets in, it illumines other things too; hidden things I'm not prepared to face.

Like hunted quarry, I'm pursued by hounds that won't let up. A tenacious guilt follows me day and night. Futility follows hard after. Like a time-bomb in a spy movie, an inner clock is triggered starting a countdown.

Dogged by guilt

Some say they find peace by going inward. I've never understood this. When I go within, I find something else. I find dark and conflicting motives. My inner child is anything but innocent. Out of my inner tumult guilt rises and pursues.

I can't get away. This dog can hunt, and it won't leave off. Day and night I hear its baying. After nightmares of being chased, I wake in a cold sweat.

I flee one way and lupin eyes seek me out. I flee another way and am cornered again. I don't know how to elude this dog. No one has taught me to offer a simple prayer of repentance.

Things were once very different. In Old Testament times worshippers offered sacrifices to rid themselves of a troubled conscience. There were different kinds of sacrifices to indicate the complex nature of sin.

A sheep or goat is sacrificed as a substitute. Symbolically, the animal's death satisfies justice, and the penalty and stain of sin is removed.

The *guilt offering* expiates. To expiate means to remove by obliterating. Sins incur a permanent debt to our fellow man and to God's justice. This sacrifice removes guilt by immolation of the offered animal.

The *sin offering* atones. To atone means to cover. A penalty is due every transgression. The sacrificed animal, unblemished and innocent, is offered as a substitute to suffer the capital punishment due the felon. This covers over sin.

The *peace offering* restores fellowship. Alienation and separation are exchanged for peace and communion.

I have no altar, no offering to sacrifice for my sin. Without expiation or atonement my guilt can only grow and fester. There's no pardon. There's no promise of renewal.

I find myself overcome by a burden that I can't get rid of. Guilt is a corrosive and toxic-waste with nowhere to dispose of it. I read of a company that tried to bury hundreds of barrels of PCBs a mile underground. A few years later it had surfaced. It had seeped through fissures in the rocks.

Guilt seeps into the cracks of my soul. Waking moments are stained with regret. Night brings no relief. Dreams are dark. Sleep is restless. I wake with a guilt hangover.

Repression becomes exhausting. Guilt takes residence— somewhere in the heart of my soul a knot is growing.

It might be psychological, but it feels physical. No amount of pot and partying eases it.

Conscience is like the little black recorder box in the cockpit of a plane. It records, rewinds, and plays back. At unguarded moments or dreams in the middle of the night, I get the replay. My inner being calls me to account. Like a dog cornering its prey, it traps, leaps and tears.

Yet, the little black box is also a homing device. At the same time as it condemns, it also beckons. Faintly but surely, I begin to hear the steady *"beep.... beep... beep".* It grows louder. Someone is calling me home.

Pursued by futility

I have dark broodings about the future. I'm disturbed by thoughts of pending nothingness, of non-existence.

My secular upbringing offers little to soothe my fears. Like most Danish Lutherans, my family doesn't abandon religion entirely. We mark birth with baptism, marriage with a church service, and funerals with a presiding minister. At the same time, no one pretends these events have any purpose beyond present utility.

When they come to Canada, after several sincere attempts to go to church, like everyone around us, my family subsides into a secular world view. Death is not talked about. The afterlife is never mentioned. I'm supposed to feel assured when I'm told "Death is just a part of life" ... or when someone close dies, "At least they didn't suffer." I didn't buy it. I'm not the only morbid teenager. Another fifteen-year-old at the time feels the same,

> *Because you were absent, the whole world seemed to me tiny and ridiculous, and the destiny of man stupid and cruel.*
> —Madeleine Delbrêl, *We, the Ordinary People of the Streets*

I am not the only morbid teenager who is inundated with a sense of impending doom. We are at the height of the Vietnam War.

The arms race is in full swing. Nuclear war looms. We are made to feel we live at ground zero—a mushroom cloud hanging over us. Pollution promises massive extinctions. A group called The Science and Security Board comes up with a global timepiece called the Doomsday Clock. It sets the time of history at ten minutes to midnight.

This dark vision is supposed to motivate change. Instead, it cements detachment, and a complete sense of futility.

> *Tomorrow, and tomorrow, and tomorrow,*
> *Creeps in this petty pace from day to day,*
> *To the last syllable of recorded time...*
> —Macbeth

An approaching nothingness casts a pall of futility on everything I do and everywhere I go. How do I respond to this?

Up to now, I've tried to throw off restraint, to anaesthetize my conscience. I repudiate moral advice as irrelevant. I use *hedonistic* logic. I reason, *"With so little time left, each day has to be filled with all the pleasures this all to brief life offers."*

I bargain with despair: *"Going to school is a necessary evil, but at least there are girls and parties to enjoy. Going to work is unavoidable, but the extra cash will fund my pleasure seeking."* Beer, pot and parties cost money.

A sincere friend asks me: "Why do you live so recklessly?" I answer, "Why not? What possible difference could it make in the bigger scheme? Everything we do ends in the grave."

Puzzled, she asks, "Can't you see what you are doing is wrong?" I answer, "Who decides what is right or wrong? Who has a right to say?" I add, "Give me a reason to fall in line—and I will. Until then, I'll make the most of the little time I have."

However full of sadness a man may be, he is happy for the time, if you can prevail upon him to enter into some amusement; and however happy a man may be, he will soon be discontented and wretched, if he be not diverted and occupied by some passion or pursuit which prevents weariness from overcoming him. Without amusement there is no joy; with amusement there is no sadness.

He who does not see the vanity of the world is himself very vain. Indeed, who do not see it but youths who are absorbed in fame, diversion, and the thought of the future? But take away diversion, and you will see them dried up with weariness. They feel then their nothingness without knowing it.
—Blaise Paschal Pensees

Nihilism fuels my hedonism for a season. Inevitably I burn out. I run out of gas. Death looming, I justify my actions, but one sin links to another, until I find myself tangled in the web of my own logic. My fear of death spurs on a reckless life, but death's futility kills the pleasure. If I give in to logic of death, it permits my self-indulgence. At the same time, the finality makes everything bitter. When futility is pitted against selfishness, futility will win every time.

I don't want to go quietly into that dark night.

A futuristic movie—*Bladerunner*—stares at death. The apex speech is spoken by a super-intelligent cybernetic robot. Roy Batty is designed to live in the hostile conditions of deep space. For decades he has traveled the universe working where no human can go. However, he and his kind are mortal- they are programmed to time out at pre-set hour. They are designed to not fear death—that is, until one, Batty, develops an awareness of his mortality.

This cyborg tries everything to avoid the futility of timing out. He locates the scientist who designed him. Meeting his maker, Batty pleads, barters, and threatens- asking to be reprogrammed. It's impossible. He can't be reprogrammed. Batty's final day is hard wired.

Recklessly, Batty takes others with him into the void. First, he kills his maker. Next, he attempts to kill his pursuer. When the policeman is hanging by his fingertips on a ledge, unexpectedly, Batty has a chance to spare a life. He ponders a new possibility. Now rescuing a life can become a substitute for him losing his life. Batty reaches out a saving hand. Now he is willing to surrender to his fate. He muses out loud. Rain glistening on his face, as last seconds tick, sorrow and pain bring out a poignant apotheosis.

> *I've seen things you people wouldn't believe.*
> *Attack ships on fire off the shoulder of Orion.*
> *I watched C-beams glitter in the dark near the Tannhäuser Gate.*
> *All those moments will be lost in time, like tears in rain…*
> *Time to die.*
> —Bladerunner 1982

We are going to time out. It's inevitable, final—and profoundly sad. At the same time, if we avoid death, we avoid life. Defy death and you can live life boldly. The human soul finds its meaning and identity in the face of death. There is no philosophy worth its salt that does not reckon with death. I must stare death in the face to discover life. It's part of my Maker's design and plan for me.

I'm guilty without an altar. I'm doomed to die, with no reprieve. But things are about to change. Out of the darkness the light of hope is about to rise.

> *The sun of righteousness shall rise with healing in its wings.*
> —Malachi 4:2

Unsought and unexpected, I am about to have another soul rending revelation. It happens one day, when I hear a voice calling me in the fog.

CHAPTER 7 • A SIREN SOUNDS

I'm hungry for drama, not the kind that is staged. The pyrotechnics of a rock concert leave me flat. I'm looking for awe. I'm about to experience it in the five-alarm intensity. Kindness and beauty will not be enough to turn me from my selfish ways. When I hear the siren blow, I know it's not just fire drill. I'm supposed to head to the exits.

Late one night, I'm hanging out a friend's house. We've been *smokin' and tokin'*—but I no longer feel the *jumping into the deep* sensation. Marijuana is just a habit. I'm pretty much played out when it comes to getting high.

We listen to Simon and Garfunkel. Good philosophical stuff. We're mellow. My friend decides to share some philosophical insights. (Robbie is one of the few deep-thinking types I know). He reads excerpts from *Memories Dreams and Reflections* by Teilhard de Chardin. He explains the concept of the noosphere, Teilhard's word for the collective human mind—a consciousness we all share and are steadily moving towards. Robbie wants to convince me there is more to life than what we see. I nod with dull comprehension.

Imagining I'm tracking, Robbie pulls out another book. This time it's the big one—a Bible. He looks me in the eye. "Let me read something to you. It's really far out. My grandmother read it to me."

Robbie's grandma is a hard-core tongues and miracles Pentecostal. She treads the path of life with determined steps and grim visage. For her, each day is next to last. She's kind of scary.

Robbie reads Matthew 24. It bursts with fire and brimstone warnings about the Second Coming. He reads the chapter slowly, one verse after another. Warning follows warning, line by line, the words gather velocity and momentum, like a tsunami heading to shore,

> *"There will be wars and rumors of war"*
> *"Many false Christs will arise. Do not follow them"*
> *"Because of lawlessness, men's love will grow cold"*
> *"One will be taken and one will be left."*

Suddenly, I hear the alarm bells. I wake up. One second, a deep fog, next a diamond clarity. Drug effects evaporate. Arrested, I'm stunned into sobriety. Like previous encounters, time stops. I no longer hear the music or what Robbie is saying. It's me and the Word. Nothing else exists. Summoned and indicted, I assent to plain truth. "The world is coming apart at the seams. I share the blame. Guilty as charged!"

My day of reckoning has arrived. Somehow, I knew it would.

"There will be wars and rumors of war." I'm already primed with an end-of-days foreboding. Vietnam, the Cold War, the arms race, news of overpopulation, pollution, nuclear holocaust and mass-starvation crowd the headlines.

"Many false Christs will arise." Eastern gurus, divine incarnations, cult leaders spring up every other week. Only months before, Jim Jones, founder and leader of the Peoples Temple, draws 909 people into a murder-suicide of biblical proportions. They drink the kool-aid.

"Men's love will grow cold." No imagination needed here. Loyalty, friendship and kindness are scarce.

"One will be taken and another will be left." This is a new concept for me—but the meaning is clear. In this cataclysmic scenario, as things stand, I will be left behind.

Words force their way in. I am powerless to disagree with what Robbie reads. I don't just hear words. I'm being spoken to. This is a revelation and everything in me succumbs.

The finale hits me like brass-knuckles. *Like the lightning which shines from the east to the west... so will be the coming of the Son of Man.*

I am seeing things I've never seen before. Imagine a fiery bolt at midnight—thunderous cracking and careening across a black sky—all 200 million volts. It's a flash and nothing can hide, everything concealed is revealed. Shadows dissolve. Only the real remains.

I hear words but I also see what the words describe. I'm having a vision. The New Testament word for vision is *orasis*. It is a soul perceived experience of divine reality. The visible disappears. Like a blinding camera flash, the words leave an after-image. Decades later, I can close my eyes and recall everything in detail. The picture is indelibly etched on the retina of my heart and mind.

I look up at Robbie. He is unaware of what has just *come down*. He stays high and dry. He finishes reading and looks at me quizzically, wondering what I am thinking.

I sit fixed to my chair, somewhere between trance and shock. On one hand, I'm terrified. Warning builds on warning, truth to the power of truth. Yet something else is happening. This is the awe I've been waiting for. It captures every cell. I hear the words of the One who forges the tectonic forces of quasars, galaxies and nebula- and who architects the destiny of humanity.

I hear the voice—loud and clear. "God is speaking to me... in this room... right now." Life collapses into an irreducible essence. It's me and God, as if nothing else exists. I find myself between hammer and anvil. When the hammer strikes, it will break open my soul. It's my big bang. Something new explodes out of nothing.

> *In the beginning was the Word.*
> —John 1:1

My thoughts careen and collide: "Terrifying"... "The end..." "Catastrophic" No propaganda, no evasion, it's up one the side, down the other. Detonated, these words can't be capped. Holy terror has been loosed.

> *"We are mixing up a batch of TNT. We should all wear crash helmets."*
> —Annie Dillard

I heed the warning. There's a chasm between me and the One who speaks. I tell myself, "John, you're in Trouble, with a capital T." I'm on the wrong side. I'm outside the coming kingdom. I know in my heart, "There will be massive reparations." If I don't heed, there'll be hell to pay.

> *"They will hide in caves and call on the rocks to cover them."*

At the same time, breaking through this maelstrom, is a profound awareness of something else—another word is being spoken to me—a new and different word- a new and different realization. If there's a way of being shut out, then there is also a way in. If there's a door that forever shuts, there must be a door that's forever open.

I hear an invitation. *"There is a day of judgment—there is also a day of pardon."* Emerging from the threat of judgment is a hope and promise. I reason, "It must be, if there's a final day, it must be there's also a tomorrow—the day after the final day." If there's an end to the world— there must be a beginning beyond it. I'm wakened by the alarm—but I also feel beckoned,

"The Spirit and the bride say 'Come.'" —Revelations 22:17

God confronts me from both sides. He warns and he invites.

I accept the scowl and seek the smile. I recognize this Voice. It's not a stranger talking to me. God has always been talking to me. The warnings and invitations have always been there. Just now, they're so loud I can't fail to hear.

> *Deep inside my heart his name remained, and nothing could entirely captivate me, however learned, however neatly expressed, however true it might be, unless his name were in it.*
> —Augustine *Confessions*

I'm ready to believe and follow- just a few more experiences and I'll know the way.

CHAPTER 8 • THERE IS SOMETHING ABOUT THAT NAME

I pretend I'm happy. I act like I'm part of the tribe. Inside, my life is slowly spinning out of control. I have an inner emptiness. Emptiness is literally nothing. This nothing grows.

I'm hoping to connect permanently with the awe. Like many of my peers, I go to rock concerts. For my generation, rock and roll concerts are supposedly the apotheosis of the human experience—our secular temple. Descriptions of the experience are almost religious, "Unbelievable!" "Far out!" "Awesome!"

Music is still a big part of my life. Some of it reaches deep. I remember the first time I listen to Led Zeppelin with earphones. I've never heard anything like it. "Whole Lotta Love" bangs from one side of my head to the other— and I love it.

One night I go with my girlfriend to see Three Dog Night. We try to get into it. We applaud. We whistle. We cheer. On cue we venerate. We move through several mandatory curtain calls. I burn my fingers holding up a cheap lighter. No matter how I try—I just can't find the ecstasy. As the concert winds down, I'm looking at my watch, wondering when it will be over. "Sure, it's kind of cool—but...but... there has to be more than this."

The soul has a ravenous appetite. A rock concert just leaves it hungry for more. So, I watch and wait.

Robbie is interested in Christianity. He is the friend who read Matthew 24 one night. He has an unusual practice. He rebukes anyone who uses Jesus Christ as a curse. Once I did and he asks me, "What is it about Jesus that makes you want to drag his name into the dirt?" It's a good question. It makes me think.

When *Jesus Christ Superstar* comes to town, I'm not sure what it is about, but I decide I need to see it. I know Jesus belongs somewhere in the mosaic of my quest. During the play, I have a mini epiphany. The word epiphany means to *bring to the light*—to enlighten. If you have an epiphany, it is like a light turns on. This time it's a stage light. It shines on the main character.

My attention is on JC, as Herod calls him. Lloyd Webber knows how to reach our emotional center. The music is good, but it's the drama that grabs me.

Like every revolutionary, Jesus goes toe-to-toe with the establishment. He draws the powerless to himself. At one point a harried crowd calls out to Jesus,

> *Hosanna Heysanna Sanna Sanna Ho*
> *Sanna Hey Sanna Ho Sanna*
> *Hey JC, JC won't you fight for me?*

When the high priest insists Jesus silence the crowd. Jesus gets white hot:

> *Why waste your breath moaning at the crowd?*
> *Nothing can be done to stop the shouting*
> *If ev'ry tongue was still, the noise would still continue*
> *The rocks and stones themselves would start to sing*

I'm not sure I've seen this kind of righteous anger before. Something about JC is different. He's not political. He's not just fighting for human rights. There's something vertical about his cause. Jesus is not about Jesus. The people want to idolize him. Jesus, doesn't get sucked in.

Like Herod, I wonder, "What gives with this JC?" The decadent and flamboyant King asks Jesus to prove his divinity, offering to free him if he does. He doesn't even reply. He sees where this bargaining leads.

This Broadway JC is compelling. He is something new—something different. He walks through the world like he owns it or, at least, knows the One who does. He speaks on behalf of God. At this pretty much secular play, I am captivated with the first brush stroke of Jesus' brilliance. Up to now I see only black and white. Suddenly I get a glimpse of color.

This encounter isn't as profound, or deeply emotional as the other revelations. Still, it's something to go on. Once again, I'm introduced to that other dimension. My flat world is becoming spherical.

I wonder why my first meeting with Jesus should be so human. I doubt the Messiah of Lloyd Webber's imagination. I conclude God reveals glimpses of Himself in echoes and shadows.

Why didn't I meet a fiery evangelist? Or get invited by a pious friend to go to church and hear a sermon? I guess I wasn't ready for a fuller picture. I was definitely not interested in subjecting myself to someone's proselytizing. Probably I needed pablum before I was ready to digest anything solid.

When the curtain falls, I can't get JC out of my mind. I think about him for weeks. I tell Robbie, "There's something going on here. Whoever this Jesus is, I'm impressed. I'm going to find out more."

I enter a new stage of my journey. It's no longer about getting high on pot or immersed in rock and roll. My quest becomes personned. It has a name-J*esus*.

CHAPTER 9 • GOING IT ALONE

> *How can people have no feelings*
> *How can they ignore their friends*
> *Easy to be hard*
> *Easy to be cold*
> *Easy to be proud*
> *Easy to say no*
> —Three Dog Night

It's not easy to find a true friend. When people live for themselves, they have little margin for others. On the other hand, if the story is true, start looking for a True Friend and you might find God is already looking for you.

At the time, friends occupy center place in my life. I try to make and keep friends. In the process, I discover the qualities that make a good friend. I put loyalty at the top. A friend is someone I can count on when the chips are down. They may not know how to help, but they know how to show up. A friend accepts me as I am—but isn't afraid to challenge me. A friend is someone I can confide in and who confides in me. If I need someone to unburden my soul—I look for a friend.

If you'd asked me at the time, and I would have told you that I have friends I can count on, that will be there for me if I need them.

At this stage, as I draw near to what I am seeking for, progress is arduous. I trudge through a thickening underbrush of guilt and regret. I need someone to care, to listen, and to help. I need a real friend.

One night I'm with my closest friends in a frequent haunt—the pub at the Trade Winds Hotel on Macleod and Glenmore. This windowless, smoke-filled dive smells like a day-old drunk and feels like a tomb. You have to down more than a few beers not to notice. Five of us circle round - tumblers of 60-cent beer cover the table—an effervescent refinery. Normally, we talk about nothing and quaff a half dozen. Afterwards, we figure to slouch behind the wheel and wander our way to a poker game, a pool hall, or to the local MacDonald's for a feed.

This night is different. I can't get into the routine. I'm bummed out—oppressed by another brew- a rising blend of guilt and anxiety sits heavy and weighs me down.

I need to leave. I need to leave now.

I didn't drive that night—so I ask my friends for a lift. These are the guys I hang out with all the time. It seems a small thing. I'm sure they'll help me out. One by one, they glance at me with a smile and nod, then drop their eyes and turn back to the beer and conversation. They hope I won't press the matter. Perhaps they don't perceive my distress, or perhaps don't really care.

I turn to Robbie. I tell myself, "He'll understand. He knows what it's like to crash and burn". When he was bummed out, I spent an entire afternoon driving him around the foothills. It was a glorious fall day. I talked him up when he was down. The colors and splendor of a sunny fall day calmed his soul.

Now it's my turn to be depressed and it's his turn to comfort.

"Hey Robbie, give me a lift. I need to leave. I'm bummed out."

"Now?" he asks. "Really?... You'll be fine."

"No, I won't."

He turns his head to look at me. His stare meets mine. He has to know something is not right.

I repeat my plea, "C'mon man..." He looks away.
Echoes of a recent song replay in my head:

Do you only care about the bleeding crowd?
How about a needing friend? I need a friend
—Three Dog Night 1969

I feel trapped in this pub. I know in my present state of mind I can't stay. I need to go somewhere, anywhere but here.

We gotta get out of this place
If its the last thing we ever do
We gotta get out of this place
—Eric Burdon and the Animals 1965

Rejected and dejected, I head to the exit. I walk home—very alone. It's only a few kilometers—but it's the longest walk of my life.

That night I discover a hard truth. It took a simple test to learn a painful lesson. Deep friendships are rare. True friends are in short supply. Few have the time. Few have the capacity. Fewer still understand what it takes.

Already depressed, now, I'm wounded. I recall the words that I heard from Matthew 24; *Because of lawlessness, the love of many will grow cold.*

There are things in the world today that harden the arteries of a man's heart. It's something about the time we live in. People have forgotten how to be friends. A kind of relational amnesia has set in. We've stopped listening to each other. We can't be bothered to make the effort to be there for a hurting friend Without hope and without faith, our individual and collective loneliness is pervasive:

He is the lonely man, and the larger the crowd in which he lives, the more isolated he is. Despite the pleasure he might derive from his solitude, he suffers deeply from it. He feels the most violent need to be reintegrated into a community,

God Seeking | 57

> to have a setting, to experience ideological and effective communication. That loneliness is perhaps the most terrible ordeal of modern man; that loneliness in which he can share nothing, talk to nobody, expect nothing from anybody.
> —Jacques Ellul, *Propaganda*

In everyday conversation, there is a narrow range of acceptable topics, especially men relating to men. Express tender affection or ask a deep question— you'll likely be met with a credulous stare. A reproachful glance tells the truth— "Hey, don't bring your inner questions here. Keep them to yourself". In shallow times it's easier to ride the surface. Talk about sports. Talk about girls. Talk about nothing.

> *A man hears what he wants to hear and disregards the rest.*
> —Simon and Garfunkel 1969

Aristotle taught, "Man is a social animal." Human existence is composed of relationships. Like blood flowing in a body, meaningful friendships keep a family, city, or civilization alive. Lose friendship and life dies.

This night, I shuffle down silent streets to my home, I realize I have to go it alone. My friends aren't ready for the journey. Others care but just don't understand. My girlfriend cares. (She will join me later) My parents care. They just don't relate to what I'm going through. If I don't understand what's happening myself—how can they?

Where I'm heading, I have to leave everyone behind. The final stage will be solitary. I now realize this is how it works. It's part of a plan. God wants my undivided attention. A spiritual quest is reduced to perfect simplicity; *"I and Thou"*.

One of God's names is <*parakletos*> it means *along-side*. (John 14:16) Looking back, I can see that God is already alongside. He meets my seeking soul one-on-one. Theologians tell us God is not scattered and diffused throughout the universe. Because God is everywhere fully present and everywhere conscious at once, He can give undivided and personal attention to each one of several billion people.

In another story, there's a traveler who goes solo. The main character's name is Christian. John Bunyan writes *Pilgrim's Progress* from a prison cell. He was thrown in jail for twelve years because he wouldn't knuckle under to the Pharisees of his day. He understood what it meant to go it alone.

It's a parable about the journey of a lost soul from the *City of Destruction* to the *Celestial City*. Along the way, Christian meets and battles gruesome characters like Giant Despair and diabolic foes like the dragon- spirit Apollyon. He is tempted to follow Mr. Legality up the unscalable mountain of self-righteousness.

At the beginning of the parable, Christian reads a book that terrifies his conscience. He tries to tell his friends and family what is happening to him. He can't get anyone to understand his inner torment.

> *I dreamed; and behold, I saw a man clothed with rags standing in a certain place, with his face from his own house, a book in his hand, and a great burden upon his back...In this plight, therefore, he went home, and refrained himself as long as he could, that his wife and children should not perceive his distress; but he could not be silent long, because that his trouble increased: wherefore at length he brake his mind to his wife and children; and thus he began to talk to them: "O my dear wife," said he, "and you the children of my bowels, I, your dear friend, am in myself undone, by reason of a burden that lies hard upon me; moreover, I'm for certain informed, that this our city will be burned with fire from heaven; in which fearful overthrow, both myself, with thee, my wife, and you my sweet babes, shall miserably come to ruin; except (the which yet I see not) some way of escape can be found,*

> whereby we may be delivered."
>
> At this his relations were sore amazed; not for that they believed that what he had said to them was true, but because they thought that some frenzy distemper had got into his head; therefore, it drawing towards night, and they hoping that sleep might settle his brains, with all haste they got him to bed: but the night was as troublesome to him as the day; wherefore, instead of sleeping, he spent it in sighs and tears. So, when the morning was come, they would know how he did: he told them, "Worse and worse."

No one understands. None are willing to head with him down the road. Christian is forced to journey alone:

> So, I saw in my dream that the man began to run ... but his wife and children... began to cry after him to return; but the man put his fingers in his ears, and ran on...

After some severe hardships, Christian has a vision of a man hanging on a cross. As he approaches, a great burden falls off his back and rolls into a deep grave.

Unburdened, Christian heads down the straight and narrow. He often falters. After each fall, he's met by Evangelist, who gives him strong words and a small book to read. He meets up with Hopeful and Faithful and they travel together for a time. Later his friend Hopeful is martyred at Vanity Fair.

Pilgrim's Progress is a parable and metaphor of everyone's spiritual quest. After the night in the pub, I don't know where to go. I only know I can't stay where I am. I've to go it alone. Like Christian, I start to run headfirst, unsure where I'm going-anywhere but here.

CHAPTER 10 • THE ENDLESS CIRCLE

I know, O Lord, that the way of man is not in himself, that it is not in man who walks to direct his steps.
—The Prophet Jeremiah

I came to seek and save the lost.
—Jesus

Imagine how a little boy felt that morning in Brooklyn. What goes through my child mind? I head down the road to find a store with hope and anticipation of enjoying a candy necklace. I have no landmarks on the trail. The hillside apartment we were staying at is indistinguishable from a hundred others. The first street I head down has no stores. Disappointed, but undaunted, I go further down three or four more streets with no luck. Then I begin to wonder if I should turn back, but not just yet. I still hope to find my heart's desire around the next corner. A few more blocks and failed attempts I reluctantly accept the fact that I'm not going to find what I search for.

Realizing my family would miss their boat if I didn't hurry, I head back. At first, optimistic of finding my way. I set out to retrace my steps. I turn a few corners and look around. Nothing's familiar. I am a little concerned but keep going. After several failed attempts, I come to a dead stop because I've got nowhere to go. Any direction I take is pointless. Forget the candy. I'm completely lost. I am also ready to be found.

This episode parallels my spiritual journey. I get lost looking for something I think I need. From age fourteen to seventeen I seek meaning and happiness through a maze of pleasure seeking. I set out bold and determined. Something cosmic and significant has been withheld from me and I mean to find it. I imagine I can find the sweetness in life. It turns out to be empty calories.

How did I get so lost? I turn to Canada's first naturalist, Grey Owl, who describes how easily someone can lose their way in Canada's wilderness. He began writing in the 1930's.

Grey Owl has the credentials for telling the story. He begins his wilderness explorations as a fur trapper. He watches his comrades wipe out indigenous populations of fur-bearing animals. His work comes to an abrupt halt when he sees a mother beaver caught in a trap, still clinging to her two kittens. It breaks his heart. Disgusted with the industry and himself, he quits the fur trade and turns his concerns into writing. Grey Owl's descriptive and humorous writing celebrates the beauty of the wilderness and exposes threats of extinction.

In *Men of the Last Frontier*, Grey Owl narrates in detail how it is easy to wander off the path in Canada's forested regions. Even seasoned woodsmen get lost, though more frequently those new to wilderness travel. If you are lost in the vast Canadian forest, the end of the trail can easily be the end of the trail.

> One day a deer hunter took an afternoon stroll and was discovered eleven days later by one of a gang of twenty-five men who scoured the woods for him for twenty miles around. In the first case the man strayed off the water-trail in the dark. He attempted to correct his mistake and took a short cut only to arrive back at the river at a different point. He again endeavored to strike the camp but angling too much to his right he missed it. So much was learned by the finding of the pail at riverbank and by his tracks. After that he entered a country of burnt, bare rocks, and small patches of green swamp, and he is there yet.

Heading out for a refreshing hike, in minutes it happens that someone becomes irretrievably lost. Grey Owl explains:

> A man may start on a bright sunshiny day, with all confidence, to make his way to some as yet undiscovered lake or river.

Inviting glades offering good traveling open up in every direction. Gulley's lead so miraculously from one to another in just the right directions; a glance at the sun affords all the indications of route necessary. The course is smooth, the wheels are greased, and he slides merrily on his way.

Having lured him in so far with fair promise, the fickle landscape now decides to play one from the bottom of the deck. The going becomes thicker during the next half hour, and the ground inclined to be swampy, with quite a few mosquitoes present... The sun guilefully seizes on this as the psychological moment to disappear. The traveling becomes worse, much worse. ... Generous and intractable hardwoods, standing close packed, with interlaced limbs, form an entanglement from the feet up, through which a man is hard set to it to force a passage. Overhead is an impenetrable mass of twisted branches, through which a perspiring man vainly endeavors to get a glimpse of the sun, only to discover it is gone.

It's no easy matter for a confused traveler to retrace his steps. The trail is just as easily lost on the way out as the way in. While an experienced woodsman takes care to commit to memory every single landmark on the way in, the newcomer neglects this survival technique. Attempting to get back to where he started, the novice finds one tree looks the same as another. Promising paths head in every direction. Even though our wanderer might be a short distance from his starting point, he loses all sense of direction. Before long he is completely lost.

When a seasoned explorer loses his bearings, he will stop and make camp. He will have a good night's rest and reassess his situation in the morning. By then, others might find him. However, the beginner is distressed at being lost. He makes hasty calculations and hurls himself headlong into the quest for his point of origin.

Grey Owl explains what happens next. It is a strange but

regular occurrence for those who are lost in the wilderness. It's called the endless circle.

> *He now, wisely, decides to eat and think it over; so, making a fire, and infusing his tea with swamp water, he builds himself a meal.*
>
> *After this, and a smoke, being now refreshed, he goes forward with renewed energy and zeal. This in time wears off; there is no improvement in the going. He would be much cheered by the sight of a familiar landmark... Presently he smells smoke. Wondering who but one in his own predicament would make a fire in such a jungle, he trails up the smoke, finding an odd footprint to encourage him; he will at least see a man, who may know the district. He arrives at the fire and no one is there, but there are tracks leading away, which he commences to follow, on the run... with sudden misgiving he sets his moccasined foot into one of the strangers' footprints, to find they fit perfectly; the tracks are his own. He has been tracking himself down to his own fireplace!*

I don't know much about wilderness exploration. However, I know a lot about being lost. I wander into my own endless circle. It starts as a promising trek, an adventure. I try different paths, each time hoping this new way will lead me closer to a fulfilling destination however, I lose my way. I get turned around and can't seem to find may way back. I've no inner compass. Before long, with sickening certainty, I realize that I'm lost.

I'm headstrong though, and don't give up easily. I still hope to squeeze the water of meaning out of the rock of indulgence. The polite word for this is hedonism. Some pursue pleasure as a mere lust. Others seek meaning in pleasure. Like me, some do both.

> *I said in my heart, "Come now, I will test you with pleasure, enjoy myself". But behold this also was vanity. I said of laughter, "It is mad." and of pleasure, "What use is it?" I*

> *searched with my heart how to cheer my body with wine—my heart still guarding me with wisdom—...I got singers, both men and women, and many concubines, the delight of the children of men... I considered all that my hands had done... and behold all was vanity and striving after the wind, and there was nothing to be gained under the sun.*
> —Ecclesiastes

I run down the untrod path without compass or landmarks, and oblivious to the danger. I don't know when to stay "stop". I have not learned how to say "No". If some is good, more must be better.

A few years of bacchanalia brings me to the end of the trail. Futility and guilt cloud my world, blocking any rays of hope.

I recall a frightening wake up call. One night I get high with a friend. We smoke. We drink. We take other stuff. Out of nowhere, I find myself in the middle of a conversation not knowing where I am, how I got there. My mind is completely blank. I must have blacked out. When I come to, I can only stare ahead stupidly and not have a clue what to say.

I'm left with a sickening realization; "this is what it means to be lost".

At this point in my journey, I'm lost—in an impenetrable forest. I've lost sight of the sun. Time and again I return to the empty futility where I started. I've run out of options. I'm trapped, defeated, and frightened. I not only don't know where I am, I don't know where to go. Unless someone finds me, I'm sure I'll perish.

Grey Owl describes the frustration of a man trapped in the endless circle. He comes back to his starting point again and again. He not only feels lost, but he also feels trapped. He wants to be found. He is desperate to get out of the endless circle.

Disappointments turn to discouragement, discouragement to dismay, dismay to despair. Now I'm desperate to break free from my aimless wandering. I'll even surrender my self-sovereignty.

Jesus tells a parable about a wayward son who gets lost. He rejects his father and family and demands his share of the inheritance before his father dies. (He doesn't have the patience to wait). He heads down the path of self-indulgence. He spends his money recklessly, depletes his endorphins, and ends up in rags of poverty. This prodigal son ends up in a far-off country, feeding pigs (there could be no greater shame for a Jew), craving the husks they feed on. He is lost to his family, his friends, and himself.

> *He longed to fill his stomach with the pods that the pigs were eating, but no one gave him anything. When he came to his senses, he said, 'How many of my father's hired servants have food to spare, and here I am starving to death! I will set out and go back to my father and say to him: Father, I have sinned against heaven and against you.*
> —Luke 15

Jesus is making a point in this parable. It turns out that getting truly lost is the necessary criteria for being found. Like this poor soul, I'm lost in a far-off country. I'm feeding on husks. Guilt outweighs pleasure. For the prodigal and for me, the trail becomes vain and weary. I wake up and realize I'm going nowhere. I'm in my own endless circle.

One thing becomes clear. I want to get unlost. Like the prodigal son, I'm ready to be found.

Before long I will find myself on another path and in another circle. I find it in a garden.

Finally, I'll be found.

CHAPTER 11 • BACK TO THE GARDEN

> *We are stardust.*
> *We are golden.*
> *And we've got to get ourselves back to the garden.*
> —Joni Mitchell

I find my destination through a path in a monastery garden.

Considering the distressing behaviors of my teen years, a psychologist might conclude that the drugs, the hormones, and the selfishness combined for a recipe of self-induced conversion. Perhaps I needed myself to be found and projected the solution.

For my part, I'm certain that similar dramatic encounters with God happen all the time. God uses the passionate searching and reckless indulgence of youth to waken a searching soul to awe.

Consider Augustine, a 5th century Latin Father. He emerges from a profligate adolescence and meets God in another garden. Walking through a courtyard with heavy steps and a burdened soul, he hears a little child say, *"Tole lege...Tola lege... Take up and read... Take up and read..."* Responding to the cryptic phrase, Augustine picks up a Bible, opens it randomly and reads, *"Put put on the Lord Jesus Christ, and make no provision for the flesh, to fulfill its lusts."* (Romans 13:13–14) Augustine ran out of the garden, beat his breast and cried to God.

At sixteen, St. Patrick was kidnapped and brought to Ireland as a slave. His bondage and youthful torments should embitter him, instead his sorrows feed love for his captors. Patrick escapes his captors only to return later to woo the Emerald Isles to Christ— king and all.

Around thirteen, Joan of Arc starts hearing voices and

experiencing visions, which she interprets as signs from God. Before long, kings and nations alike heed and follow her into holy war.

In his youth St. Francis of Assisi was renowned for drinking and partying. While a soldier fighting in a battle between Assisi and Perugia, Francis is captured and put in prison for ransom. He spends nearly a year in jail—awaiting his father's payment. According to accounts, while in prison Francis begins receiving visions from God. After his release, Francis hears the voice of Christ commanding him to repair the Christian Church and live a life of poverty. In obedience to the call, he abandons his life of luxury and becomes the apostle of the poor.

Like these saints, I am amazed how God uses the good and the bad to bring me to Himself. I detect the purposes of God. I tread the path to perdition because I need to. I've had four awakenings because I need each one.

My own garden experience brings these revelations together and seals my conversion.

After graduating, I work to save money for the big trip to Europe. This is the one thing I've been looking forward to for years. Two friends say they are committed to join me but backout at the last day. That's another story.

While saving for the journey one summer day, I'm working with Luigi, an Italian cabinetmaker. We head out to install counters and benches at a Catholic monastery across from *Cemetery Hill* just south of downtown Calgary. I didn't know this place existed.

During coffee break, I walk up the hill to look around. I come upon a cultivated garden. It's the cool of the day. Resplendent in summer array, a bewildering variety of flowers adorn the bushes. Shrubs are laden with roses through the garden.

Placed at intervals along the path are statues and a cross. They are set back from the path, leaving room for visitors to stop and contemplate.

As I enter through the path, I experience an encompassing calm. It's not just that the wind dies down, the spatial and temporal atmosphere changes. Everything seems to belong here. Part sacred, part natural—the garden and saints are in harmony.

As soon as I enter, I'm drawn in. I experience a complex of curious sensations. I've crossed some sort of boundary. This garden is its own little world. When lunch break is over, I linger for a few minutes. When I go back to work, the garden sensations stay with me through the rest of the afternoon.

The past few years, I've had moments of timeless revelation—Saturday in the church basement, the symphony of stars, the apocalyptic reading from Matthew's gospel, and Jesus Christ Superstar—but these moments subside into memory. Until this day, the revelations haven't gained the mass or momentum to penetrate the wall of my ignorance and self-will.

I've been troubled in heart and mind for some time. The hound of guilt pursues. I feel a chronic anxiety much of the time. Resigned to my lost state, I wander in circles, with no sense of direction.

Søren Kierkegaard calls this condition *angst*:

> Anxiety is being 'afraid' when there is nothing to fear. We struggle with something in the dark, but we don't know what it is. From somewhere and yet nowhere seeps out a vague feeling of threat. Floating around in our body, unsettling our stomach, a generalized sense of menace possesses our whole being. This uneasiness has no identifiable cause. Our anxiety is seldom an object of consciousness that we can focus on; rather, it seems to be a deep, inner state of our being, which makes itself felt without the aid of conceptual thought—indeed against our

> *fervent wish to be free of anxiety. In angst we confront the fundamental precariousness of existence; our being is disclosed as unspeakably fragile and tenuous. And when it bursts thru the protective shell in which we try to encapsulate it, our anxious dread renders us helpless.*
> —Søren Kierkegaard 1844

Angst finds residence within. I recall it with painful vividness. Angst is not so much a something as it is an emptiness. It is a problem with no solution, a question without an answer. This emptiness has different names- anxiety... loneliness... futility... dread. Deep down is a fear of death, a fear of being cast out, a fear of life without a tomorrow. It is a fear of life without God.

> *Above all he is a victim of emptiness—he is devoid of meaning. He is very busy, but he is emotionally empty, open to all entreaties and in search of only one thing—something to fill his inner void.*
> —Jacques Ellul 1962, *Propaganda*

For months this angst has been with me every waking moment—and in every nightmare. I take it wherever I go. It forms a knot in my gut.

The Greeks talk about a *Gordian knot*. It is a peculiar knot. It can't be undone. Pull at it or even try to untie it, it simply gets tighter. My knot is Gordian. I can't escape it. I want desperately to rid myself of it. If I try to evade it, it tightens all the more. Like some kind of malignancy, it is embedded within. This knot might be psychological, but it feels physical. It sits in the middle of my chest—about the size of a racquet ball—and hard as Indian rubber.

This soul-grinding anxiety will turn out to be my salvation. The pain has a hidden purpose—it drives me from self in all its forms—self-will, self-determination, self-adulation—and leaves an empty space for God to fill.

Learning to know anxiety is an adventure which every man has to affront if he would not go to perdition either by not having known anxiety or by sinking under it. He therefore who has learned rightly to be in anxiety has learned the most important thing.
—Søren Kierkegaard 1844

It's late afternoon and the working day winds down. It's *quittin' time*. We gather our tools and sweep the floors. As we get ready to leave, Luigi asks if I'd like a lift home. We are buddies. He's worried for me. He can see I'm troubled. There's no bounce in my step, no smile on my face. The old John is nowhere to be found.

I tell Luigi, "Go ahead. I'm just going to hang around a bit."

I head up the hill—me and my inner knot.

After work, on a nice day, I often head to nearby Stanley Park to share a six-pack or even a dozen beers with a companion from high school. Garry and I would sit by a bend in the Elbow River, drink and talk about women—and stuff. Lately, I pass. I no longer get a buzz from the beer. I've no energy to spare for the aftermath of my indulgences. It just tightens the knot.

I stick around the monastery. I head up the hill to explore the garden one more time. As I approach the entrance, I can see the path is a circle, entering and exiting at the same place. Taking my time, I head in. I wander slowly through. I've got no other place I need to be. Every few steps I pause to look around, to smell the fragrances, to listen to the quiet.

Like earlier that day, I experience a surrounding calmness. I can't name it, but I can feel it. Something about this place... something safe... something friendly—even welcoming... The garden is filled with life—not just flowers and bushes.

I enter with a restless mind, ceaseless anxious thoughts, and fretting.

Annie Dillard describes our busy consciousness:

> *The mind wants to live forever, or to learn a very good reason why not. The mind wants the world to return its love, or its awareness; the mind wants to know all the world and all eternity, and God...Further: while the mind reels in deep space, while the mind grieves or fears or exults, the workaday senses, in ignorance or idiocy, like so many computer terminals printing out market prices while the world blows up, still transcribe their little data to the warehouse in the skull.*
> —Pilgrim at Tinker Creek

The minute I enter the garden, my anxious thoughts dissipate. The inner monologue ceases, I become part of the moment. As my mind stills, I'm suspended in a calm and sacred awareness: This garden is more than flowers and fragrances. There is Peace in this place. There is Presence.

The garden is inhabited by an Invisible and Radiant Fulness. I'm drawn in. In fact, I can't draw back. I don't want to. I never want the moment to pass. I could stay in this place—maybe for a year—maybe forever.

Before I enter my soul is a storm. This place is tranquil. Before I enter, my heart feels barren. This garden is filled with life. Before I enter, my mind is in chaos. The garden blooms and grows with ordered freedom.

I see it. I feel it. I want in.

I continue to walk the path, wandering slowly in, around and through. I notice the design. Trees, shrubs, greenery, flowers are intentionally positioned along the way. Nothing is random or out of place. Statues of the saints emerge from green shrouded enclaves. Plants shade the trail. Colors and fragrances merge.

I'm the only one in the garden—but I don't feel alone. Unlike the void in my heart, this garden is filled with something. It is *Personned*.

Winding my way through, I notice the statues. Every few meters a different saint, then Mary, and then—wouldn't you know it—Jesus. I recall his statue has open arms. I don't recall if the arms are open because he is nailed to a cross or because he is ready to embrace. Maybe it's both. This statue doesn't dominate the garden. It surveys it.

Awed with crowding thoughts and feelings, I know I am encountering something utterly new and different but at the same time familiar. It seems strange, but it makes all the sense in the world. I'm coming back to where I belong.

The world is not an empty place. It's more than the colliding of unseen atoms. God inhabits the creation he made. If we have eyes to see, He is everywhere—entire, conscious, and present.

> *In him we live and move and have our being.*
> —St. Paul, Acts 17

Slowly it dawns on me that I'm a guest in this garden—invited or summoned- an audience of one.

As I make my way deeper into the garden, I'm aware I'm being spoken to. God's words do not have to be spoken. They just are. Nothing is audible, yet the voice is clear. I'm invited to reply.

> *The silence is all there is. It is the Alpha and the Omega. It is God's brooding over the face of the waters. You take a step in the right direction to pray to this silence...*
> —Annie Dillard

It's more than me and the garden. The ground is holy. I stop and collapse to my knees. I break the stillness and pray aloud: "God,

I'm wrecked. Broken. Please heal me. I'm all misery. There's a knot of unhappiness in my gut. I've tried everything—but I can't get rid of it. If you take this away from me, I give my life to you. If you heal me, I will give my life to others who feel the same despair."

Even as I cry out, the knot disappears. I feel it untie, lift, and disappear. In a timeless moment, it is gone. The angst—the emptiness, the guilt and anxiety, are gone—entirely, at once, and forever.

That very instant, Something Else takes residence.

This emptying is a filling. Something new comes into me—something Other. It is spiritual, not ethereal. The filling is so real that a physical sense of peace pours over me, rising to an inner awareness. I stay on my knees to savor and to ponder.

How can I describe what I feel like in this moment? "Relief...relief...relief"—a thousand-fold *relief*.

The previous winter, I sprained my ankle skiing. Someone says, "Leave the boot on. Your foot might be broken." The ankle swells double—with nowhere to go. Ski boots have no give. I experience pain like never before. I'm ready to faint. It takes an hour to get to the hospital. As soon as I enter, the doctor removes the boot. The pain explodes away. *"Relief...relief...relief."*

In this garden, I offer a simple prayer. Like letting go of some dark claw—relief explodes. I draw a deep breath. Imagine the first breath of a newborn. A pardoning embrace permeates the emptiness. The healing balm sooths the wound left by the knot. I'm enveloped, inhabited, and immersed in an inner peace.

I know it is God who meets me in the garden. I recognize Him from the other revelations. It was God that passed by while I studied catechism. He was there in the singing stars. God spoke to me in the fog. I recognize His echo from my inner world—the homing device of my little black box.

Up till now it has been a one-way conversation. Now two-way contact has been made.

> *By praying I believed that God found me and that he is a living reality, and that we can love him in the same way that we can love a person.*
> —Madeleine Delbrêl

I'm not sure how long I've been in the garden. It might have been an hour; it might have been a few moments. Encounter eternity and time departs. At the same time, what happens to me in the garden will take a whole lifetime to unpack. I don't have words to explain it at the time, just a palpable and undeniable experience of forgiveness. My emptiness is cast out—never to return. The house is swept clean. Something new takes residence. I'm filled by God. I'm filled with God.

This plentitude replaces the old and dead. In place of loneliness, there is belonging. Instead of futility, there is purpose. Instead of despair, there is hope. I see light rising on the horizon—illumining a new path, leading to a new tomorrow.

Rising from my simple prayer, there is a new song in my heart—full-throated and suffused with joy.

POSTSCRIPT

As high school years end, a defining event occurs. I know it's from God. He has architected a plan.

A Christian high school club has organized a concert. Power and Light is the Band. They go from high school to high school sharing the gospel through music. Hallway gossip is out— "It's a Christian thing." Some roll their eyes. A few are curious. Some want to go but fear their peers. Most hear the propaganda and stay away.

At the time, I have no Christian friends—at least the kind that let me know. The only public-type Christians I know of are Sandee Dean and Dee Antliffe. They stand out and they stand their ground. Sandee is homecoming queen. She gives thanks to Jesus for winning. That draws some snickers. Dee is attractive in quiet and gracious way. She's shy but somehow, we all know she follows Jesus. Pretty much everyone respects these two women—even while they keep their distance.

We save our derision for closet Christians. I recall a conversation with my brother, Ole. Early each Sunday we drive to the Rockies to ski. One day, on the way to the slopes of Lake Louise, I share my contempt. "How can church-going Christians pretend to know God? If they really believe they can live forever, why don't they lay their lives on the line? Why aren't they more reckless?"

Then I put out some dangerous words. "If I knew there was a

God, I would stop at nothing to change the world. If I believed in God, I would throw myself into the cause. If I knew I could live forever—nothing could stop me speaking up and giving up everything". Brave words. I'll soon have to live them or eat them.

When I catch wind of the noon-hour Christian concert. I'm more than curious. I'm cautious but I don't want to stay away. I need to tell someone about my God meetings.

Leaving lunch friends behind, I head down the hall and walk by the gym—*nonchalantly*. Clashing drums and singing tells me concert is well under way. I screw up courage to peek.

I enter the back of the gym. The place is pretty much empty. No more than thirty listeners mill about. *"The few. The brave. The Christians."* There's no one I recognize, at least no one popular. I think, "Good. No one who matters will recognize me".

I stand at the back—behind the stacked bleachers. I glance around the corner to listen and to see what's happening. I remind myself of another closet believer. Nicodemus is a high-ranking religious leader. He wants to meet Jesus, but not publicly. He's afraid of losing his reputation with his peers and his privileged status among the people.

Under cover of night, Nicodemus finds Jesus and opens the conversation. He starts with a compliment. He says, *"Rabbi, we know that no one could do the works you do unless God were with him".* —John 3:2

Jesus doesn't bite. He cuts to the chase: *"Unless you are born of the flesh and of the Spirit you cannot enter the Kingdom of God."* —John 3:5

Jesus means, "Let go of your old life, Nicodemus. Your reputation. Your status. Your influence. It's counterfeit currency. You need to get rid of the old and ask God for the new.

Come out of hiding, God will rebirth you so you can live forever. Hang on to your old life—you will forfeit the Kingdom of God and miss the One you wait for".

Jesus words sink in. Later, we find Nicodemus comes out of the closet. He stands up to the supreme council leaders when they plot to kill Jesus. He protests their trumped-up charges. After the crucifixion, he wraps Jesus' body in costly, fragrant spices.

That noon hour, I skulk around like Nicodemus. From behind the bleachers, I see the stage clearly. *Power and Light* is a band of two guys and two girls. I notice they have long beautiful hair. They're laughing, dancing, and singing their hearts out. You would think they were playing a packed house. They're layin' it down—with passion.

They remind me of another musician who was heedless of self:

> *David was dancing before the LORD with all his might, while he and all Israel were bringing up the ark of the LORD with shouts and the sound of trumpets.*
> —2 Samuel 6:14 -15

They don't draw attention to themselves—the personal acclaim thing. They play for the few that gather. They also play for the other Audience—the Unseen One. In this empty gym, Power and Light is all about the music, the song, and the One they sing for. One tune after the other, I hear a new sound. Unlike the minstrels of mayhem, I am familiar with, they are troubadours of joy.

Song after song, the music gets stronger, happier, and tighter. It's fun. It brings happiness to my heart. I don't know what they have—what power, what light. I love their laughter. I respect their courage. What they have, I want.

When the concert ends, and the gym is emptying, I come out

from behind the bleachers. The way to the front is clear. I make a beeline to the stage. "These guys will understand. They'll relate. I've got to talk to them." I haven't told anyone what God is doing in my life. I'm dying to tell someone.

Coming up to the guys, I notice the girls, they're beautiful. They carry themselves with a modest happiness. Their smiles have an unfeigned and irresistible ambiance. They exude a physical and spiritual harmony. There is something sacred within them that makes me look at them with simple affection.

I approach the lead singer. As he puts instruments and microphones away, I say, "Hey I really like your music. You guys are really good".

"Thanks!"

I blurt out my story—the Coles notes version. "You know, I'm really going through some things now. I think I've met God. I feel like I have to tell someone. I've got to do something."

He beams, "Wow. That's great man. Like what happened?"

I give him a brief tour of my quest—reading about the apocalypse, the stars, and the prayer in the garden.

I tell him I'm on my way to Europe for a post-high-school trip. I have a ticket that permits me to stay up to a year. "I'm thinking of going to Israel and becoming a missionary or something." I have no idea why I believe this. I assume that's what converts are supposed to do—go to a foreign country and start telling everyone about God.

He encourages me. "Hey man, that's great."

I'm thrilled to finally tell my story. I feel completely safe with this stranger- somehow, I know I can trust him. He seems like he knows a lot about God.

He offers a few suggestions. "Read the book of James. It has a lot of solid stuff about justice and righteousness."

"Okay, I will."

He adds, "And when you get to Europe, look up Youth for Christ International. We work with those guys. The head office is in Geneva. They'll help you on the next steps of your journey".

I hang on to his words. I'm counting on this being a guiding word from God. It turns out to be so.

I'm ready for a fresh start. I have the first stage of my roadmap. I read James, many times over. James' prophetic call to justice and faith echoes through my whole life.

When it comes time to head oversees, I get the gear I need. I have a full knapsack and an unused bible I find on a shelf. My girlfriend, Caron, also gives me a guitar for the trip. I pack my bible. I strap on my guitar. I grab a few LPs by Carole King, James Taylor and John Lennon—mellow minstrels to smooth a frayed soul. I head off to Europe—the land of my forefathers and the next place for my songs and prayers.

After visiting relatives in Denmark, I go to Geneva and meet the Youth for Christ team at their offices. They direct me to a Christian community in the Swiss Alps called L'Abri. It means The Shelter. I'll spend four months there learning about prayer and about what it means to follow Jesus. My time at L'Abri shapes my journey- profoundly.

I can't see the future, but the dread of tomorrow is gone. A new adventure beckons—a path bright with hope.

God will meet me again. Only this time, I'll be looking for him. Fifty years later I'm still on the hunt.

www.ingramcontent.com/pod-product-compliance
Lightning Source LLC
Chambersburg PA
CBHW071012160426
43193CB00012B/2018